Reflections

Twenty Biblical Characters

by various writers

GW00471115

All royalties for this book going towards the **Robert Morrison Project**, a Christian organisation working for Christian revival in the growing Asian church

DayOne

First published in Great Britain in 2021 by
Day One, Ryelands Road, Leominster, HR6 8NZ
Email: sales@dayone.co.uk
Website: www.dayone.co.uk

Scripture quotations marked (ESV) are taken from The Holy Bible, English Standard Version (ESV®), copyright © 2001 by Crossway, a publishing ministry of Good News Publishers. Used by permission. All rights reserved.

Scripture quotations marked (NIV) are taken from the Holy Bible, New International Version®, NIV®. Copyright © 1973, 1978, 1984 by Biblica, Inc.™ Used by permission of Zondervan. All rights reserved worldwide. www.zondervan.com

Scripture quotations marked (NKJV) are taken from The Holy Bible, New King James Version (NKJV®), copyright © 2001 by Crossway, a publishing ministry of Good News Publishers. Used by permission. All rights reserved.

Scripture quotations marked (NASBRE) are taken from The Holy Bible, New America Standard Bible (Revised Edition) (NASBRE), copyright © 2001 by Crossway, a publishing ministry of Good News Publishers. Used by permission. All rights reserved.

The views expressed in this publication belong solely to the authors and do not necessarily reflect the opinions or views of its affiliates.

British Library Cataloguing in Publication Data available

ISBN: 978-1-84625-706-3

Cover design by Kathryn Chedgzoy

Printed by 4edge

Chinese Visual 1930—
Chinese text translates as
'Old and New Testament'

Contents

Twenty Biblical Characters

Acknowledgments

The editors would like to proffer our indebtedness to the writers of this compendium of short narratives of Biblical characters. The task set was to write on or about a favourite character of their choice but set inside very tight parameters. Our thanks go to these budding authors for their expertise and indeed whetting our appetite to read and study the word more, that God's name will be glorified.

Many contributed by their encouraging comments, suggestions, proofreading, and general support of this project. To all we give a big thank you and apologise for not mentioning the numerous individuals by name, except for Stanley's wife Naomi Millen, who we are indebted to for typing and photocopying.

We would also like to thank the directors, editors and the whole team at Day One Publications, particularly Mark Roberts, managing director.

Stanley has a great burden for Christian revival in China and, therefore, would like to support the Robert Morrison Project through this book. Those at the Robert Morrison Project, '... believe it is vital that reformed churches worldwide take proactive steps to meet the literature needs of the growing Asian church.' Their desire 'is not to replace the development of indigenous authors, but rather to supplement their work by publishing some of the most influential reformed authors in church history.'[1]

Royalties will go to: robertmorrisonproject.org.

Stanley Millen

Daniel McKee

Introduction

COVID-19 has tried to cover many things in its global sweep. It has tried to cover knowledge of Christian Revival in China. The reader should read Tony Lambert's book, *China's Christian Millions* (Monarch 2008), to be informed and inflamed, in order to pray for revival in this country.

COVID-19 has also tried to cover individual characters as it sweeps across communities and nations. The Bible, on the other hand, is full of individual characters, some named and others unnamed.

There are eighty named characters in Nehemiah 10 and thirty-two in Romans 16. At the same time, there are unnamed characters like the blind man in John 9 and the cripple in Acts 3.

In the following pages, we have named writers, writing about named characters of the Bible (Old Testament and New Testament). They were invited to write about characters that challenged and encouraged them.

Finally, and most importantly, there is a name that is above all other names, 'that at the name of Jesus every knee should bow, in heaven and on earth ... and every tongue confess that Jesus Christ is Lord, to the glory of God the Father' (Philippians 2:10, 11 ESV).

Adam

Chapter 1

Adam is the First

A dam is the first human we meet in the Bible, a man who was unique with many privileges. Created by God and placed in a perfect world, he was made in the image of God; but what does this mean?

Adam was more than a collection of random molecules. He was not just body; he was also soul/spirit. Adam, like God, could communicate in language, not mere instinct. With language, he could reason, discuss and communicate ideas. He was infinitely above the rest of creation. He was able to have fellowship (Genesis 1:28). God was creative in an incomparable sense; he was able to create out of nothing. He created the universe when there was only himself, the Triune God. Adam too was creative, but not from nothing. He used the gifts God had given him such as music, or the use of tools. With this creative gift, humans can design all manner of art, music and structures. Animals cannot do this—for example a bird never re-designs its nest; it is the same year after year.

Adam was also moral

Adam was also moral; he had the sense of right and wrong. He had true holiness and righteousness. God gave him a perfect partner, Eve, to be his helper. She too was made in the image of God. Both lived in a perfect garden which they were to care for, and could use their creative ideas in. They were to have children and live to God's glory. One special law was given: they were not to eat of one tree, the tree of the knowledge of good and evil (Genesis 2:16–17). The tree was made special by God's command—otherwise it was an ordinary tree. The penalty for eating from it was spiritual and physical death.

Enter Satan

Satan came in disguise under the cover of a snake. His aim was to encourage Adam to disobey God. He was an intruder in the garden and should have been put out, but instead the couple listened to him. He began to question the word of God (Genesis 3:1b). Eve listened; she was taken in by him and took the fruit. Adam, who was with Eve, knew this was an act of rebellion. He acted wilfully.

Adam lost his true ...

Adam lost his true holiness; his morality was twisted. He lost fellowship with God. The other aspects of the image were not lost but distorted. Now his creative gifts were used for good and evil. Sin engulfed the human race, since we are all descendants of Adam. We all experience spiritual and physical death. Was there any hope?

Another Adam to the Rescue

Yes! Christ came into the world, known as the last Adam (1 Cor. 15:45). He was fully God and truly human; he was without sin. He was tempted by Satan in the wilderness but did not give in; he lived a perfect life. He represented the fallen human race, living for them, and on the cross he experienced divine wrath for sinners. He rose on the third day and ascended to glory. Now any sinner, who trusts him, is forgiven; fellowship with God is restored and he becomes a child of God. The first Adam messed it up. Praise God for the last Adam who gives hope to all who trust him.

William McKeown

Elihu

Chapter 2

A very imperfect messenger of God (Job 32–37)

When I think of Elihu, I am tempted to remember Benjamin Disraeli's rather unkind but colourful description of William Gladstone: 'A sophisticated rhetorician, inebriated with the exuberance of his own verbosity, and gifted with an egotistical imagination that can at all times command an interminable and inconsistent series of arguments to malign an opponent and to glorify himself.'[1]

'I am full of words'

Is this fair? In entering the lists with Eliphaz, Bildad, Zophar and, of course, Job, who have already covered thirty chapters in hot debate, Elihu was certainly declaring himself to be a rhetorician. Nor is his tendency to verbosity much in doubt. He says of himself 'I am full of words' (Job 32:18), a sentiment which few of his readers would deny. Is he egotistical? In the first chapter of his discourse, he uses the pronoun 'I' nineteen times, and 'me', 'my' and 'mine' thirteen times, and his claim to have wisdom superior to the older participants would certainly give his readers reason to suspect so. As to the description, 'interminable', it has to be noted that once he starts, he doesn't draw breath for a full six chapters. Some commentators have described him as 'endless Elihu'.

Elihu was ignored

So, what are we to make of Elihu? Is it not likely that the vacancy hearing committee would report to the Kirk Session[2] that his application be ignored? In fact, in a sense this is what happened. Elihu was ignored. When he eventually finished (37:24), neither Job nor Eliphaz, Bildad or Zophar make any comment whatsoever, and we never hear of him again. Elihu is a very imperfect messenger of God. Could it be that God has given him this slot in his Word so that Christians, and especially Christian leaders, would cry out with David, '... see if there be any grievous way in me?' (Ps.139:24 ESV).

Has Elihu any good qualities?

Now, in spite of Disraeli's description of him, Gladstone, with all his failings, achieved a number of very positive reforms under his premiership. But what about Elihu? Has he any good qualities; anything to teach us; anything for us to emulate? In the first place, it is clear that he is a very good listener. He has listened well to the earlier participants in the debate and is well able to sum up their arguments. In this too, he exhibits considerable ability in that he quotes verbatim some of what Job has said.

Elihu declares the majesty of God

But let's not also forget that, underlying the thoughts and feelings of the messenger, there is a message—a message of good news. Elihu, for all his ramblings, declares the Majesty of God, and his Sovereignty in all things. He speaks of how God, in his great love, uses the difficult providences of life to cause repentance unto salvation. And, most importantly of all, in those very early days— for the book of Job was probably the first written word of God—he introduces us to a 'mediator' (Job 33:23 NKJV), a 'ransom' (Job 33:24 NKJV), a 'redeemer' (Job 33:28 NKJV).

As we look at Elihu, is it not challenging and also encouraging to know that God takes such an imperfect preacher and uses him to declare his Word?

Ian McCleen

17

Esau

I have a real fondness for Esau. I can imagine him as a real man's man who would have been good company. A sportsman who loved the simple things of life, like a good meal at the end of a day's hunting with friends. His father, Isaac, loved him like nobody else; he was his real pride and joy.

But Esau settled for much less in life than he should have. Here is this son of Isaac, this grandson of Abraham, 'the father of the faithful' (see Galatians 3:7–9 NIV), and he sells his birthright for a bowl of stew after a day in the fields.

'I have enough' (Gen. 33:9 ESV)

Even at the end of his story in God's big story, we read of him telling his trickster of a brother Jacob, 'I have enough' (Gen. 33:9 ESV). He was satisfied with his foreign, idol-worshipping wives and family, his wealth and possessions. That was enough.

He had no thought of the birthright he had sold; the blessing of his father Isaac, of which he had been robbed. No thought of the God of Isaac and Abraham; of a nation through whom all the nations would be blessed; of the promised seed who would one day restore the world as it was meant to be.

Jacob thinks Esau is going to wipe him out. After all, they had not met up for years, since Jacob had tricked their father and had received the blessing of the elder son.

So, Jacob protects what is nearest and dearest to him and offers Esau generous gifts in the hope that his brother will not murder him. And Esau responds with forgiveness and generosity—'Look Jacob, I have enough!' Yes, I am fond of Esau, and feel quite angry at his conman brother Jacob.

But I'm tragically missing the point. Esau has enough without God. He's happy to live life as what we might call today *a thorough-going secularist*. Family, friends and material things are enough for him; there's no thirsting for anything more.

I've met a lot of 'Esaus'
I've met a lot of 'Esaus' in my life: kind, generous people who are good company, many of them hanging around the edges of church life; decent hardworking people who are satisfied with far less than God's best for them. 'I have enough. Why would I ever need to follow Jesus Christ?'

'See to it that no one fails ...' (Heb. 12:15 ESV)
But my opinion of Esau is far less important than that of the Lord's. We read these terrible words:

> See to it that no one fails to obtain the grace of God; ... that no one is sexually immoral or unholy like Esau, who sold his birthright for a single meal. For you know that afterwards, when he desired to inherit the blessing, he was rejected, for he found

20

no chance to repent, though he sought it with tears (Heb. 12:15–17 ESV).

No hope for Esau, but still hope for us. For the grace of God is offered freely to us through our Lord Jesus Christ. Today the Saviour offers us salvation, eternal life and a new friendship with Him and all his people.

Hope

Was there hope for Esau's tribe? Well, that's another story. It's the story of a young girl called Ruth and a child born from her descendants—the Saviour of the world!

Graham Connor

Joseph

Chapter 4

Joseph knew all about setbacks

Joseph knew all about setbacks. He lived a roller-coaster life: the pampered favourite of his father, Jacob; hated by his jealous brothers; thrown into a pit to slowly die; then sold into slavery far from home in Egypt; falsely accused by his master Potiphar's wife; cast into prison; forgotten by Pharaoh's butler whom he'd helped. Psalm 105:18 NIV tells us:

> They bruised his feet with shackles, his neck was put in irons.

This can also be translated as 'his soul was laid in irons'. Emotions of betrayal, pain, fear, humiliation, injustice and despair pierced his inner self. These experiences turn many a person into twisted, bitter, vengeful people. Joseph, however, weathered the storm. He kept his integrity. He treated others with humanity, though he was treated inhumanely. He forgave his brothers. In a time of famine, he settled them and his father, Jacob, in the plenty of Egypt. He became the saviour of Egypt and the surrounding lands with a wise food-supply policy.

Joseph is a fruitful vine

In later years, Jacob said of him: 'Joseph is a fruitful vine ... whose branches climb over a wall,' and revealed his secret: 'A fruitful vine near a spring' (Genesis 49:22 NIV).

Joseph was rooted firmly in God from whom he drank deeply. He was not ashamed to speak of his faith, even to Pharaoh, who perceived in him, 'the spirit of God' (Genesis 41:38 NIV). By that Spirit, he was enabled to show remarkable forgiveness to his brothers. Joseph's difficulties seemed senseless, but God was in them. He saw that though his brothers, '... intended to harm ... , God intended it for good ... the saving of many lives' (Genesis 50:20 NIV).

The Christ, who, like Joseph ...

Centuries later, Jesus stopped by Jacob's well in the countryside that was bequeathed to Joseph. There he said:

> Whoever drinks of the water that I will give him will never be thirsty again. The water that I will give him will become in him a spring of water welling up to eternal life (John 4:14 ESV).

He invites us to drink, to follow and to be rooted in Him —the Christ, who, like Joseph, was persecuted, despised, sold for silver, and cast into oblivion.

The cross of Jesus shattered the disciples and proclaimed the power of his enemies but: 'It was the LORD's will to crush him' (Isaiah 53:10 NIV).

The crowd at the cross of Jesus considered '... him stricken, smitten by God, and afflicted' (Isaiah 53:4 ESV).

The prophet and the gospel declare:

> He was pierced for our transgressions; he was crushed for our iniquities; ... the LORD has laid on him the iniquity of us all (Isaiah 53:5–6 ESV).

In him we have redemption through his blood, the forgiveness of sins. (Ephesians 1:7 NIV).

And we are called to bear the likeness of Christ.

One-time Moderator of the Presbyterian Church in Ireland,

> I have looked with wonder at Niagara Falls, and the grandeur that is the Alps. I have been in rapture over the beauty that is Scotland's mountains and the wonder of the Portrush waves, but I acknowledge ... the surpassing sight of all things here below—the beauty of Jesus, wrought in a human life, in the midst of a busy life.[1]

The testimony of Christlike living is powerful still.

Donald Patton

Moses

The view from Mount Nebo

Sir Francis Drake having crossed the Panama and standing in a tree on a high ridge of land he glimpsed the Pacific Ocean and prayed that he 'besought Almighty God, of His goodness to give him life and leave to sail once in an English ship in that sea.[1]

In the providence of God, his wish was granted and surely, he died content, having realised his ambition. He did all he planned to do. Not all are so blessed.

Moses, for forty years, led and taught the people of Israel. His story was full of highlights, involving palace life and education, shepherding, husbanding, political leadership and being the spokesperson for the Divine to a recalcitrant generation. As his life neared its end, he had led the nation to the verge of the Promised Land, which he had been forbidden to enter but viewed it from Nebo's lofty height (Deut. 34). Away on the horizon he could see the Great Sea; to the north lay snow-capped Hermon and Galilee. It went ill with Moses at Meribah (Nu. 20:2–13) and God ruled that he would see the Promised Land of the patriarchs but he would not enter it. Unlike the English sailor, his wish was not granted.

What Moses accepted

As the Civil War was drawing to a close and it was clear the north would prevail, President Lincoln was aware of the toll that conflict had taken on his health. To an adviser he said, just a few weeks before he died:

> I have read these strange and beautiful words several times, these last five or six weeks ... Now I see the end of this terrible conflict, with the same joy of Moses, ... But just as the Lord heard no murmur from the lips of Moses, when He was told that he had to die before crossing the Jordan, for the sins of his people, so I hope and pray that He will hear no murmur from me when I fall for my nation's sake.[2]

This episode in the life of Moses highlights the reality that limitation is part of human existence. There is pathos in the fact that Moses, in the moment of triumph akin to Nelson at Trafalgar and General James Wolfe on the Heights of Abraham, all passed away in the moment of their glory.

What Moses achieved

The godliness of Moses is seen in this; he accepted the divine will, without whining. To dwell unduly long on the limitations of life could deflect us from this truth: how much good has been accomplished. Moses had brought his people to the verge of victory, given them a moral code and a worship pattern which lasted until the Messiah came, and established them among the nations for all time.

Nothing became Moses in life as his leaving of it. He bowed to God's plan (Deut. 3:23–29); was recalled by succeeding generations as one who knew God face to face (Deut. 34:10); and trained Joshua to carry on his work. Here is a legacy any servant of God would envy.

Arthur Clarke

Caleb

Everyone is concerned with being young and healthy and this fascination has even made its way into the church. I want to point you to a man who at eighty-five years of age was as fresh mentally, physically and spiritually as he was at forty.

Caleb had a different spirit

According to Numbers 14:24 NIV, 'Caleb has a different spirit.' Caleb, son of Jephunneh, stood on God's promises while his fellow spies said:

> We can't attack those people; they are stronger than we are ... The land we explored devours those living in it. All the people we saw there are of great size ... We seemed like grasshoppers in our own eyes, and we looked the same to them (Num. 13:31, 32, 33 NIV).

As the people were getting themselves in a frightened tizzy:

> Caleb silenced the people before Moses and said, 'We should go up and take possession of the land, for we can certainly do it' (Num. 13:30 NIV).

Caleb had faith against all odds, that God would deliver on his promises, so God said,

> Because my servant Caleb has a different spirit and follows me wholeheartedly, I will bring him into the land he went to, and his descendants will inherit it (Num. 14:24 NIV).

31

Yet to the rest, God spoke these words, 'Not one of you will enter the land I swore with uplifted hand to make your home' (Num. 14:30 NIV). Forty-five years later, Caleb was back ready to claim the promise that God had made that day, and enter Canaan. Even though now eighty-five, he was as keen now, as he was back then to take hold of God's promises. His main concern in life was God's assessment.

You too have a different spirit

Whether you are eight or eighty, the main thing is that you too have a different spirit. We are all born with the same spirit spoken of in Ephesians, 'As for you, you were dead in your transgressions and sins' (Eph. 2:1 NIV). We are all born in sin and with a desire to keep on sinning, and that brings us into direct conflict with God who is sinless and can't allow us into his sinless presence. It means that we are out of step with God in this life and that we will be separated from him eternally in the next life. But, like Caleb, we too can have a different spirit. And that comes about through turning to follow God and accepting his forgiveness for our sins. When we do this, we can know we are changed, as John tells us, 'We know that we live in him and he in us: He has given us of his Spirit' (1 John 4:13 NIV). When we come to know Jesus personally, his Holy Spirit lives in us and that makes the greatest difference to how we live. Caleb had a different spirit from all those who were around him, and that made the greatest difference to how he lived.

Caleb stood on God's promises

Caleb stood firmly on the promises of God and he was convinced that they could take the land and make it theirs. His faithfulness in God's Word didn't waver over the forty-five years, as, at eighty-five years of age, Caleb stated his claim, 'Now give me this hill country that the LORD promised me that day' (Josh. 14:12 NIV). He was as keen today to lay hold of God's promises as he was back forty-five years before. God's Word was God's Word and Caleb knew he could rely on it and trust it. When Caleb stood on God's promises he was able to look down on the giants who lived in Hebron. The view from God's promises gave Caleb a different perspective on what looked like a perilous situation. As a man who should have been on the old-age pension for twenty years says, 'So here I am today, eighty-five years old! I am still as strong today as the day Moses sent me out; I'm just as vigorous to go out to battle now as I was then' (Josh. 14:10–11 NIV). I'm sure there aren't too many that could say that at eighty-five, but mentally and spiritually we need to be unwavering when we are trusting on the promises of God.

Owen Patterson

Abigail

Chapter 7

1 Samuel

Jesus said, 'Blessed are the peacemakers' (Matt. 5:9), and we find a notable example in 1 Samuel 25—Abigail, wife of Nabal; a wise and beautiful woman married to a brutish man. David's men have been providing protection for Nabal's shepherds and David asks for hospitality as a reward. Nabal scornfully dismisses the request. In anger David, with 400 men, sets off to slaughter Nabal's entire household. The matter is reported to Abigail. Now watch with admiration her peace-making achievement.

She was proactive

She was proactive—she lost no time in formulating a plan and taking decisive action. No victim mentality or fear held her back. Abigail accepted responsibility and showed initiative. People like this change the world and get things done.

She had a proven track record.

She had a proven track record—the desperate servants came to her, obviously believing that she might be able to save the situation. They had witnessed her wisdom, grace and effective intervention in difficult situations—a learned skill.

She was prudent and resourceful

She was prudent and resourceful. Hiding the plan from Nabal, she prepared a vast supply of food and drink to bring as a gift to David. She used what she had—the basic principle of stewardship.

She was a positive and practical problem-solver

She was a positive and practical problem-solver—she did not sit and wring her hands, or only pray—though I am sure she did pray. She formulated a plan and put it into action. Experience and faith had made her a woman of hope.

She was amazingly brave, humble and wise

When she met David, she was amazingly brave, humble and wise. She bows with her face to the ground, honouring David, to make reparation for the insult heaped on him by her husband. She starts on the right note. Honour, not condemnation.

Then she falls at David's feet and, in a Christlike act, offers to take the blame for all that has happened, although she is entirely innocent. She apologises for her husband's ingratitude and unkindness. As a mediator and protector, she is prepared to sacrifice herself for her household.

She speaks the truth plainly

She speaks the truth plainly about her evil husband—a necessary aspect or part of any healing and peace-making.

She preaches the gospel

Finally, she in effect preaches the gospel—she asks for

forgiveness and blesses David with provisions. Then she proclaims that God is with David and David will one day be king (1 Samuel 25:28). She exhorts him to trust in God for protection and says that, if he refrains from his rash plan for vengeance, he will not have this needless bloodshed on his conscience in later life. In these moments she takes on the role of a prophet and a counsellor. Abigail doesn't just rebuke David's folly, but she enables David to see how restraining himself would benefit his long-term future. She takes the long-term view—a key component of wisdom.

Reflecting some of the Great Peacemaker's own wisdom and love, Abigail, in this her sole Bible appearance, is a gem worthy of our admiration and attention. David saw her worth and when Nabal died of shock after hearing about all this, he took Abigail as his second wife.

David Cupples

Elijah

For me personally, Elijah has always stood out as both a challenging and encouraging figure from the Old Testament. These adjectives might almost seem to be self-contradictory, but they are not, because Elijah, like all of us, was a complex character in many ways.

Elijah was a man just like us

I think that sometimes we seem to see historical figures as somehow *different* from us: a bit *two-dimensional*. But, as James reminds us in his epistle, 'Elijah was a man just like us' (James 5:17[1]), with all our feelings and emotions. So, when we turn to 1 Kings and consider Elijah's experiences and his responses to them, there's a lot that we can learn about our society and, more particularly, about ourselves—both as an encouragement and as a challenge.

We will be well aware of the state of the kingdom in Elijah's day. God's chosen people had forsaken the covenant and were lusting after the false gods of the alien people, among whom they were living. Even the king had forsaken his high calling! King Ahab had been led astray and the people had followed. The society looked, by the outward appearance, to be prosperous at that time. But under the surface it was rotten; the standards of God had been forsaken. We need hardly take time to labour the point about the parallels in our own day in Western societies, given, as they say, 'the times we are in'. The similarities are self-evident at a time when every man does that which is right in his own eyes (Judges 21:25).

Elijah appointed

God's response is to introduce into this situation the prophet Elijah. We know nothing about his background, other than that he came from Tishbe in Gilead. It is not important. We do not need to know. I recall a colleague of mine many years ago—a man long since deceased—who said this: 'When God wants to speak into a situation, he appoints a man, he does not appoint a committee.' God, in his sovereignty, appointed Elijah to proclaim the Word of the Lord. His name meant *the Lord is my God*, and essentially that was his message in the face of the opposition that he encountered from the priests of Baal and Asherah. What is clear is that Elijah had a relationship with God that was fully trusting. We could learn a great deal from his patience, waiting on the Lord. He waited until it was God's appointed time to make the next move—and then reacted. Another lesson for us surely: how important it is to understand God's timing, when we should act and how we should act—in Elijah's case, by word and action, to utterly oppose the false worship and God-rejecting standards in that nation. Parallels again, surely, with our own day.

Elijah rose to the challenge

Elijah rose to the challenge. We are well aware that, in our own day, our Christian faith and proclamation is under attack, sometimes openly, but more often orchestrated in subtle and cynical ways. It seems unbelievable to those of us who can compare the situation to that which pertained forty or fifty years ago. But that is today's reality. Is our response the response of an Elijah? I have said a number of times from the pulpit that, 'there is no such thing as a cringing Christian cowering in a corner'. As we sometimes sing in Robin Mark's song, these being the days of Elijah.

Elijah knew that God is in control—yet

And yet, it doesn't quite end there, does it? We cannot begin to imagine the *high* that Elijah must have been on immediately after his—or rather God's—great triumph on Mount Carmel. We read in 1 Kings 19:3 NIV that, as a result of Jezebel's threats, Elijah, this great prophet of the Lord, 'was afraid and ran for his life.' This is where the encouragement comes in. We know that God is always in control. Elijah knew that. Yet he was afraid. Elijah was a very complex and very human person. Just like us—all of us, in one way or another. Which one of us has not at some time felt confident, under God, in what we undertake? And which one of us has sometimes felt like Elijah in 1 Kings 19? There had been a psychological reaction, and from being on that *high*, he had suddenly dropped into despair. There was clearly an element of depression there (we find it also

41

in Luther, of course, and in Spurgeon in the nineteenth century, and in many others—maybe even ourselves sometimes). There was also a degree of self-pity: 'I have had enough, LORD' (v. 4 NIV) or 'I, even I only, am left, and they seek my life' (v. 14 ESV). Interestingly he'd actually got it wrong at that point—God says, in verse 18, 'I reserve 7,000 in Israel who have not bowed the knee to Baal.' Elijah was not alone. But when things go wrong, as they sometimes inevitably will, perhaps we too can feel like Elijah at that point. And that is where the *encouragement* comes in. This is recorded for a reason.

Elijah—ready yet again

Elijah was a man like us, as James has reminded us in James 5:17. More than once the Lord comes and asks the question: 'What are you doing here, Elijah?' (v. 9, 13). And Elijah is restored and is ready yet again to follow God's directives, and get back to the spiritual battle—just as we often need to be reminded of this same thing.

So, challenge and encouragement in the life of Elijah, melding together as an example to us. There's a lot we can learn from Elijah, both for our personalities and for our calling. For, are these the days of Elijah, when we can and should proclaim the way of the Lord?

Jim Gordon

Elijah

Obadiah

O badiah? The prophet who wrote the book of Obadiah towards the end of the Old Testament?

Obadiah—a pen pusher

No, this Obadiah was a pen pusher more than a prophet. He gets 15 verses in 1 Kings 18 in the middle of Elijah the prophet's conflict with King Ahab.

Wasn't he a compromising pen pusher, working as a close aide to a corrupt and idolatrous king?

Obadiah—a devout believer

There's a clue in his name which means *servant of the Lord.* 'Obadiah was a devout believer in the LORD' (1 Kings 18:3 NIV). He had served the Lord from his youth (18:12). While he served Ahab, he also protected one hundred of the Lord's prophets from being murdered by Queen Jezebel (18:4).

In the middle of the account of Elijah as the great action hero out on his own, there is no harm in learning that there were others serving the Lord. In the next chapter, Elijah, while suffering with depression, is told by the Lord that there were 7,000 left in Israel who had not worshipped idols. Obadiah was one of those 7,000.

Obadiah ... flustered and fearful

Obadiah was flustered and fearful about bringing a message from Elijah to King Ahab but we should honour his honesty and be encouraged. If the Lord can use a

45

depressed Elijah and a flustered Obadiah, can he not use us? I love the contrast between the two servants of the Lord. One size does not fit all.

At the end of John's gospel (John 21:18–22), Peter has just been told that his life following Jesus will not end easily—imprisonment and execution. Peter then points to John and says, 'What about him?' (v. 21). Jesus tells Peter not to bother about John: 'You must follow me!' (v. 22). Paul says something similar in Romans 14:3–4, addressing tension between those who felt free to eat anything and those who felt eating some kinds of meat was a compromise. What matters is not what the other person is doing or not doing but what we are doing on the path that God calls us.

Obadiah—one of those

Some Chinese Christians accept the restrictions of the authorities and worship in a state registered church—they are like Obadiah, working inside the system. Others, who cannot accept the restrictions, worship in the underground church—they are like Elijah, working as outsiders. Could both ways be right?

The co-existence of Elijah and Obadiah suggests that God, in his wisdom, may use both approaches and that both have their strengths and weaknesses. The danger for an Obadiah, on the inside, is the temptation to compromise, blurring the difference between believer and non-believer. The danger for an Elijah, on the outside, is the temptation to isolation and depression—to see ourself as the only one left.

Quiet Obadiah

With whom do you instinctively line up? The no-holds-barred Elijah, or quiet Obadiah, saving one hundred lives unobtrusively?

When you consider 1 Kings 18, John 21 and Romans 14, the main thing is to respect those who take a different path and yet are still following the same Lord, whose purposes are worked out through both.

John Farís

Joel

Chapter 10

Who was Joel?

The answer is, we really don't know. Tucked away in among the Minor Prophets is a short book bearing his name.

Some say he was a priest from his use of language, yet, he doesn't mention a king, nor does he talk about the Temple. For me, this makes the person of Joel, and the book attributed to him, a wonderful and awe-inspiring mystery.

It's wondrous that something so mysterious in its origins can be so clear in its message. We may wonder who exactly Joel was, and to whom he originally spoke, but we cannot fail to see what he wanted them, and us by extension, to firmly grasp.

Joel paints the unfashionable picture of the judgement of God

Joel paints the unfashionable picture of the judgement of God. God will not leave sin and wickedness unpunished but will come with terrible wrath. The image is one of locusts—so many the light of the sun is blacked out—coming to eat and destroy all in sight.

The prophet calls on the people to 'Wake up!' (Joel 1:5 NIV) and see the truth of God and the awfulness of sin. However, he does not leave them without hope but seeks to inspire them to remember that God has also promised wonderful things.

Joel wants the people to remember God, repent, live and flourish in his name

God, in his graciousness, has declared that through repentance there is forgiveness, restoration and a relationship with him to be enjoyed. This is what Joel wants the people to do—remember God, repent, live and flourish in his name.

That call of Joel is as important to us as it was to the people back then. Repentance is not solely a one-time deal—a one-off event at conversion—but a lifestyle of remembering God and turning to face him. As we repent in an ongoing fashion, we seek more of God as we honestly ask him to help us with our weaknesses and build us up in newness and righteousness. Repentance is a turning away, a desire to leave our sins behind us. It is not easy but God uses it to transform us, bit by bit, into that which reflects more of the image of Christ.

Joel has always inspired me to do two things:

- *Remember who God is.* He is a God of wrath and judgement who hates sin, but who is gracious and faithful to his promises to forgive and restore those who would come to him in faith.
- *Remember who I am.* I am a fallen, broken, sinful person who needs the power and love of God in my life more and more. I am someone who needs to be honest about my weakness and, through repentance, find help to grow in God's ways.

Praise be to God for Joel and his book—for the reality that it delivers and the hope that it shares. Even someone like me can find forgiveness and restoration through the wonder that is repentance and spectacle of God's amazing grace.

Edward McKenzie

Gabriel

Iwonder how you would feel if you encountered an angel? If this were to happen to me and I could pick my angel, I would pick Gabriel.

I have long been fascinated, challenged, and encouraged by Gabriel and his messages. Gabriel appears four times in Scripture. He is probably one of the 'ten thousand times ten thousand' angels (Dan. 7:10) that Billy Graham called 'God's Secret Agents'[1]. Most of these agents are unnamed and invisible to humans; sometimes they are visible in human form; occasionally they appear in their dazzling, amazing, wondrous glory.

Peace and promise

Gabriel means *mighty one of God*. He is known as the messenger of peace and promise. What a name to have! I love to read about him; to ponder on his messages. Gabriel stands in the presence of God and speaks the very words of God.

Wisdom and understanding

Daniel, remarkably, met Gabriel twice. From God's presence, Gabriel brought him messages of wisdom and understanding. In confusing situations, I often imagine what it would be like to have Gabriel come with similar messages. Then I am reminded that God has already provided such words through Scripture, the Holy Spirit, and his Church.

Birth of John the Baptist

Gabriel came to Zachariah with God's message that his wife would have a baby. This baby would be John the Baptist. Zachariah was afraid; who wouldn't be, in Gabriel's sudden presence? I sometimes think I would not be afraid; somehow, I imagine it would be like meeting a much loved, though awesome and magnificent, friend but perhaps, if it should really happen, I too would fear. Even though Gabriel assures Zachariah that his message is coming from God Himself, Zachariah finds the message incredible; he is overcome by doubt. Because of this Gabriel tells him, 'Now you will be silent and not able to speak until the day this happens' (Luke 1:20 NIV).

Yet with these stern words I sense a gentleness of purpose. Gabriel was giving Zachariah time to overcome his doubt and the promise would still be fulfilled in his life for God's glory. I find this really encouraging. When I am overcome by doubt, fear and quavering faith, God will patiently still work 'all things ... together' (Ro. 8:28 ESV) for my good and his Glory.

The coming of the Messiah

Perhaps most well known and loved is the story of how Gabriel, the Mighty one of God, appeared to Mary, announcing the coming of the Messiah. What a marvellous thing God did in Mary; what an astounding messenger God sent—the messenger of peace and promise. This magnificent creature, Gabriel, the message-bringer from the presence of God, spoke to Mary—a simple, godly young woman. Mary's response seems almost matter of fact in light of the enormity of her circumstances: 'May it be to me as you have said' (Luke 1:38 NIV). At that, Gabriel left.

It is unlikely that Gabriel will appear to tell me God's plan for my life but, through his Word, God instructs me how to follow, trust and honour Him. Mary's encounter with Gabriel challenges me to be malleable in God's mighty, all-powerful hand.

I often wonder what Heaven will be like. I know I will see Jesus, the Lamb of God. I also look forward to seeing Gabriel, the Mighty One of God.

Roberta Moore

Simeon

Chapter 12

God always has his people

G od always has his people no matter how dark things appear to be. There are times when things seem spiritually very dark with much carelessness and outright unbelief, but God still has His people. So it was when Jesus came into the world. One of these people was Simeon.

> Now there was a man in Jerusalem called Simeon who was righteous and devout. He was waiting for the consolation of Israel and the Holy Spirit was on him (Luke 2:25 NIV).

Simeon was righteous and devout

In the midst of much unrighteousness, Simeon was righteous and devout. He may have been overlooked and unnoticed by many people but he was not overlooked and unnoticed by the Lord and now, with the birth of Jesus, that new day had arrived.

Now the time had come when the Spirit moved Simeon to go into the temple courts at just the right time. He would see the Messiah and not just see him but take him up in his arms. He praised God:

> As you have promised, you may now dismiss your servant in peace. For my eyes have seen your salvation. (Luke 2:29–30 NIV).

Simeon understood

Simeon understood, by the Spirit, the nature of salvation:

'Your salvation, which you have prepared in the sight of all the peoples, a light for revelation to the Gentiles and glory for your people Israel' (Luke 2:30–32).[1]

Simeon knew the Messiah

Simeon knew that the Messiah would not be a nationalistic warlord who would destroy Israel's enemies, but the Saviour of all who would put their trust in Him, regardless of nationality or religion.

And it seems that Simeon was given a glimpse of the cost of all this. Did he in some way see the cross? He saw the division between those who would believe and those who would not believe and the anguish that Mary would endure:

> This child is destined to cause the falling and rising of many in Israel, and to be a sign that will be spoken against, so that the thoughts of many hearts will be revealed. And a sword will pierce your own soul too (Luke 2:34–35 NIV).

God always has his people

God always has his people, no matter how dark things appear to be—people like Simeon, filled with the Spirit and trusting in Jesus.

Brian McMillen

Simeon

Nathanael

Chapter 13

Gift of God

Nathanael gets a relatively brief mention in Scripture, but what is recorded of him has brought the gospel of grace home to my heart powerfully. His name means *gift of God* or *given by God*, and the short account of his first meeting with Jesus (John 1:43–51) highlights God's generous grace beautifully.

Nathanael's prejudice

What we first read of Nathanael, it can be a painful window into our own hearts. On hearing Philip's enthusiastic announcement that he had encountered the Messiah, Nathanael's answer was withering: 'Nazareth! Can anything good come from there?' (John 1:46 NIV).

Without having so much as met Jesus, he was willing to dismiss him merely on the basis of the town he came from.

Don't we often make the same mistake?

Don't we frequently make the same mistake? Often, we don't get so far as to openly say it, but aren't there times when we are unfairly dismissive of others? We might not fall into the crass sins of racism or misogyny, but isn't it all too easy to judge others without giving them anything close to a fair hearing? All too often, reading Nathanael's story has exposed my own prejudices.

To his amazement, Nathanael then discovered that Jesus knew things about him no one else could have known. The reference to being under a fig tree (v. 48) is rich with Old Testament allusion and significance. Even without delving into such details, we can see that Jesus' awareness of Nathanael being under the fig tree was evidence of Jesus' own identity. That's why it drew the great response:

> Rabbi, you are the Son of God; you are the king of Israel (John 1:49 NIV).

Here's where the gift of God comes in

Here's where the *gift of God* comes in. If Jesus knew all about Nathanael being under the fig tree, isn't it reasonable to suppose that he also knew what Nathanael had said when Philip brought him the news? Isn't it surely the case that he knew all about Nathanael's prejudice towards Nazareth, and towards Jesus himself? Yet look how graciously Jesus dealt with him! Rather than take him to task about his mistaken views on Nazareth, Jesus hailed him:

> Here truly is an Israelite in whom there is no deceit (John 1:47 NIV).

Jesus went on to give him great gospel promises (verses 50 and 51).

Of course, this doesn't mean that Jesus condoned or excused Nathanael's prejudice. Doubtless letting him see that the Messiah did in fact come from Nazareth was a challenging and correcting of his prejudice. It is doubtless too, as Nathanael walked with Jesus during his remaining days on earth, that he was often corrected when the need arose. Yet Jesus dealt with him in a truly tender and loving way. He deals with all his people this way, exposing our sin and graciously rescuing us from it. I'm glad he deals with me like he dealt with Nathanael! He truly is the gift of God.

Andrew Conway

Joseph
of Arimathea

There are a number of Josephs in the Bible. In the Old Testament we have Joseph, the son of Jacob, and in the New Testament we have Joseph, married to Mary. There is also Joseph of Arimathea, who is less well known, even though he is mentioned in the four Gospel accounts.

Who is this man?

Who is this man? What do we know of him? He was obviously from the Judean town of Arimathea but we only read of him in the city of Jerusalem. He was a rich man (Matt. 27:57 NKJV). One sign of his riches was his own hewn tomb (Matt. 27:60 NKJV). He was also a religious man, described as a prominent member of the council (Mark 15:43 NKJV).

There is something more to Joseph and it is the key to an understanding of his role on the day that Jesus was sentenced to death and crucified. Matthew tells us that Joseph was a disciple of Jesus, while John tells us something similar, adding the qualifying clause, '... but secretly, for fear of the Jews ...' (John 19:38 NKJV).

Riches and religion were not enough for Joseph and neither should they be enough for us. Where and when Joseph became a disciple of Jesus, we do not know, but it had happened and we will see how it influenced him on a decisive day.

A bold witness for Jesus

At daybreak the council met (Luke 22:66 NIV). We assume that Joseph was present as he did not consent to their decision and their action (Luke 23:50–51 NIV). This decision would be the decision to crucify Jesus. Here was a prominent member of the Council going against the consensus of his religious colleagues. The secret disciple was no longer afraid of the Jews but had become a bold witness for Jesus.

Towards evening on the same day, he carried his bold witness through as he went boldly to Pilate (Mark 15:43). He had no fear of the Roman governor, who was surprised to hear that Jesus was already dead. Pilate had the Roman centurion check that Jesus was indeed dead before he gave the body to Joseph.

A good example of Christian discipleship

John tells us Joseph was accompanied by Nicodemus, another member of the council. His time with Jesus is already recorded in John ch.3. Scripture does not tell us of the steps involved in taking the body of Jesus down from the cross. As disciples, we can imagine how tenderly and sensitively they handled the body of their Master!

The spices were supplied by Nicodemus while Joseph supplied the tomb where the body of Jesus was laid. The last act of Joseph recorded for us in scripture is this: 'He rolled a big stone in front of the entrance to the tomb and went away' (Matt. 27:60 NIV). Where he went to, we do not know, but we do know that he leaves with us a good example of Christian discipleship.

Stanley Millen

Barnabas

Chapter 15

Son of encouragement

The character I wish to highlight is Joseph.

Not the son of Jacob, nor the husband of Mary, but the Joseph mentioned in Acts 4:36.

The apostles nicknamed Joseph, 'Barnabas' because he was a 'son of encouragement'.

Isn't that a great name to be known by? Rev Eric Alexander used to have a Clerk of Session who was his *Barnabas*. Every Sunday he had something positive and uplifting to say to Eric at the church door after worship. One day Eric preached the worse sermon he had ever delivered and thought, 'If my elder says something good about that address, I will know to discount every other generous thing he has ever said to me in the past!'

Encourager

Shaking his hand following the service, his Clerk of Session said, 'Good text, Eric. Good text!'

That's the kind of encouragement we all need.

That's the sort of encourager we all need to be!

Barnabas encouraged his sisters and brothers by his generous spirit. He sold a field and shared his money with those who were in need (Acts 4:37). Touched by the generosity of Christ who had given his life in order to save him, Barnabas freely gave his resources as an expression of offering his life back to God. No one is encouraged by stingy people!

Encouragers go out

But Barnabas's generosity extended beyond finance. When the leaders of the church in Jerusalem heard that a great many Greeks had believed and turned to the Lord (Acts 11:19–26), guess who they sent to investigate? And when Barnabas saw the evidence of the grace of God, '... he was glad, and encouraged them all to remain true to the Lord with all their hearts' (Acts 11:23 NIV). Everyone is encouraged by those who sense God at work and want to bless others in their new-found faith!

How easy it is to hear good news and either say nothing or worse, to have a critical spirit or cynical heart. Encouragers go out of their way to look out for people to build up and situations to bless. John Stott[1] tells how, after he came to faith in Christ, Eric Nash wrote to him once a week for over five years, provoking and encouraging him to grow in grace and knowledge and love of the Saviour.

Encouraged the new Gentile believers

Benjamin West, the neoclassical painter and founder of The Royal Academy, tells how he became an artist. One day his mother left him in charge of his little sister Sally. He discovered some coloured ink and, in order to amuse her, Ben started to paint Sally's portrait, creating a terrible mess in the process. On her return his mother gasped but looked beyond the splodges and, picking up the paper, said, 'Why it's Sally'. She smiled and kissed her son.

West reflected: 'My mother's kiss made me a painter'.[2]

Having encouraged the new Gentile believers, Barnabas went on to look for Saul in Tarsus and for a whole year they met together with the church and taught a great number of new Christians in Antioch.

And the reason why Joseph was a *Barnabas*? Acts 11:24 gives us the answer, which ought to encourage us too: 'He was a good man, full of the Holy Spirit and faith' (NIV).

Frank Sellar

Ananias

On his way to Damascus to continue his persecution of the followers of Jesus, Saul of Tarsus was encountered by Jesus, Himself. This life-transforming moment left him blinded and dependent on others to bring him into the city, where he found himself accommodated at Judas' house on Straight Street.

Simply a disciple

A follower of Jesus called Ananias lived in Damascus. He was not an apostle and does not appear to have been an official in the Christian community. He was simply a disciple living an ordinary life in the normality of the city. But he was evidently a man whose profession was matched by his practice, as he consistently lived out his commitment to the Lord and his Word. He was also highly regarded by the Jews who lived in the city (Acts 22:12 NIV). They knew Ananias to be a follower of Jesus who, in Jewish eyes, was a criminal, a heretic and a blasphemer. Yet his own life of integrity and trustworthiness had an enormous effect on those among whom he lived and worked, and they respected him.

The Lord knew of his faithfulness and readiness

Not only had Ananias made an impression on them but the Lord knew of his faithfulness and readiness to serve Him. So, God told him to go to the house where Saul was and minister to him. Ananias' immediate reaction was a natural one as he pointed out who Saul was and what awful harm he had done to Jesus' followers, and why he had come to Damascus. Surely, what the Lord was asking him to do was suicidal—giving himself up to the murderer of his fellow believers. But the Lord tells Ananias that Saul is going to be a witness to both Gentiles and Jews and that it would be costly for him. That removed any question from Ananias' mind. Probably not fully understanding all that was happening, he trusted the Lord and, in willing obedience to his will, went to Saul.

He greets him as 'Brother Saul'

On entering the house and seeing Saul's blindness and weakness, Ananias might have been tempted to rebuke Saul for his past misdeeds and pour out righteous anger on this persecutor of the Church. But what Ananias does and says is quite amazing. He greets him as 'brother Saul' (Acts 9:17 NIV). What an impact that must have had on Saul, that this enemy should call him, 'brother'. Then Ananias lays hands on him. Saul had come to lay cruel murderous hands-on Ananias and others in Damascus but the hands that are laid on him are gentle hands of brotherly love.

Now brothers in Jesus

None of that would have been easy for Ananias but, by it, he was acknowledging that the grace of God, who had saved him, had also saved Saul and they were now brothers in Jesus. Whoever the Lord had forgiven, Ananias had no right to condemn and whoever the Lord had chosen, he had no right to reject. All that took place that day in that house evidenced grace and love and forgiveness.

Ananias challenges us to live consistent lives, to be ready to obey the Lord whatever he asks us to do and learn to forgive as we have been forgiven.

John Lockington

Lydia

This story of Lydia in Acts has always intrigued me. It teaches so many basic Christian doctrines.

Lydia had an open heart

God's *grace* brought Lydia to faith. God used how Lydia spent her time: the Sabbath day; the place she visited; a riverside where prayer was made; the friends she had; and her personal attitude—a *God-fearer*, interested but not committed to Judaism—all to lead her to hear Paul preach and to bring her to faith in Christ. God's grace took the initiative in Lydia's conversion. He moved her in that direction. The upshot was equally striking: 'The Lord opened her heart to heed the things spoken by Paul' (Acts 16:14 NKJV). Lydia had an open heart.

Lydia experienced justification

We wrongly invert the order and talk of opening our hearts to the Lord. The Bible puts it the other way around. God opens our hearts to obey the Scriptures. That is how salvation comes about. The Lord opens our hearts through the Word: that is his work. We obey the gospel, repent, and believe: that is our part. Lydia experienced justification.

Lydia and her household were baptized

God's *covenant* helped Lydia grow in grace. Paul's words had obviously proved Jesus to be Israel's Messiah. Lydia, interested in becoming a Jewish proselyte, became a Christian believer. She received Christian baptism and all its demands (see Matthew 28:18–20). 'When she and her household were baptised ...' (Acts 16:15a NKJV). That both Lydia and her household were baptized, as Cornelius before her and the Philippian jailer after her, also harks back to Jewish covenant principle.

Lydia experienced sanctification

The credibility of Lydia's faith was matched by a desire for assurance of salvation. Her offer of hospitality, given in insistent terms, combined with her plea to be adjudged a true believer, marked Lydia's growth in grace. She wanted to know more of the Jesus she had trusted as Saviour. Lydia's open heart led to an open life. Lydia experienced sanctification.

Lydia experienced service

God's *power* equipped Lydia for service. Luke ends his story with this postscript: 'So they went out of the prison and entered the house of Lydia; and when they had seen the brethren, they encouraged them and departed' (Acts 16:40 NKJV). Lydia's home became both a missionary base for the apostles and a meeting place for the infant Philippian church—the church in her house. Lydia, an ex-patriot from Thyatira, became Paul's first convert in Philippi. God had redirected Paul to Macedonia, through a vision, for that very reason. God was moving the gospel from Asia to Europe and Lydia was pivotal in that. Lydia experienced service.

Small wonder Paul wrote to the Philippians: '... for your fellowship in the gospel from the first day until now' (Philippians 1:5 NKJV). He probably had Lydia very much in mind. God's grace brought Lydia to faith. God's covenant helped Lydia grow in Christ. God's power equipped Lydia for service. Lydia had an open heart, then an open life and, finally, she became an open door—justification, sanctification, service—intriguing story indeed.

Harry Uprichard

Demas

'Demas, because he loved this world, has deserted me and has gone to Thessalonica.' (2 Tim. 4:10 NIV).

W hat a sorry story lies behind that simple sentence. The apostle Paul was now an old man, nearing the end of his life, locked up in a prison cell. He feels in his bones that the end is near and soon he will suffer a martyr's death. How calm he is in the face of it all (vv. 6–8). But he gives us a very human picture as well. Paul was lonely; he missed his books; he longed for his friends. Most of all he was troubled about one particular friend—Demas.

Demas was a deserter

The Bible doesn't tell us much about Demas. In his letter to the Colossians he gets barely a mention. In a list of greetings from those who are with him, Paul writes, 'Our dear friend Luke, the doctor, and Demas send greetings' (Col.4:14 NIV). And, in the letter to Philemon (v. 24), Paul simply describes him as a fellow-worker. Not much to go on to obtain a picture of Demas. However, at least we know that he was with Paul and shared in his work for the Lord Jesus. But not any longer! Now he was a deserter. He had turned his back and gone away.

There is nothing so disheartening to a Christian leader, and nothing so grieving to Jesus, as the person who once professed to love and serve Him, and then turns their back and deserts from discipleship. Jesus himself knew what that was like! There was a time when the crowds flocked to hear him, yet many lacked any staying power! Even the seventy whom he sent out two by two disappeared, until there were just twelve men left. 'Then Jesus said to the twelve, "Do you also want to go away?"' (John 6:67 NKJV). On the eve of the cross, one betrayed him, another denied him, and, apart from John, they all forsook him and fled.

All through the centuries, there are people who once followed Jesus, but then forsook him. What do we make of such deserters, such backsliders?

In some cases, is it that they have never been truly converted at all? More often I suspect, it's simply that they've grown cold in their love and careless about their worship. They've compromised their standards, disengaged from the life of their local church and dropped out of doing anything meaningful for Jesus. No longer is he at the centre of their lives. They act no differently to friends and neighbours who do not make a profession of faith at all. But why was Demas a deserter? What was the cause of his backsliding?

Demas the worldling

It was because Demas had fallen in love with this present world that he forsook Paul and deserted the cause of Christ. That's how it is, again and again. Worldliness is anything I love more than Jesus. It isn't necessarily something wicked or immoral. It may be my family, my friends, my hobbies, my sport, my reputation. It can be clothes, privacy, holidays, my own fireside—anything or one that matters more to me than Jesus.

What's the answer to the problem of worldliness? Is it to stop loving the world? You'll never manage to do that, you know. There's only one answer. Turn back to Jesus and confess to him your sin and failure. Allow him to forgive you. Let his love take hold of your mind and heart, so that you may be fired with a new love for him. Here's a poem I once learned:

> Come back to where you left him,
> and you will find him there
> He is waiting by the bedside where
> you used to kneel in prayer
> You are older, sadder, broken.
> You are tired of self, 'tis true.
> Come back to where you left him.
> He is waiting there for you.
>
> Anon

Godfrey Brown

Timothy

Chapter 19

'Is that okay, young man?'

'Is that okay, young man?' I like hearing that because, I think, that phrase, 'young man', no longer accurately describes me!

But when I think of one Bible hero, I think of some of our young readers of this book. 'Let no one despise you for your youth, but set the believers an example in speech, in conduct, in love, in faith, in purity' (1 Tim. 4:12 ESV).

Might I too

Many years ago, the young man Timothy reached out from Scripture, tapping me on the shoulder and encouraging me to persevere in Christian faith. Just as I was then, he was a young man. Yet the great General Paul is recorded encouraging young Lieutenant Timothy not to be overwhelmed by older people but to encourage them in Christian graces. More than that, this great apostle Paul has entrusted God's word to young Timothy. And God's word is to be guarded and proclaimed, even though the world deserts it (2 Tim. 4:1–5). Might I too—guard and proclaim the word.

Meet Timothy ... alongside others

When we meet Timothy, we tend to do so alongside others. We encounter him, for example, alongside Paul and Silas on Paul's second missionary journey:

Paul came also to Derbe and to Lystra. A disciple

was there, named Timothy, the son of a Jewish woman who was a believer but his father was a Greek. He was well spoken of by the brothers at Lystra and Iconium (Acts 16:1–2 ESV).

Paul wanted Timothy to accompany him, and he took him and circumcised him because of the Jews who were in that place, for they all knew that his father was a Greek. We also encounter him as he joins Paul writing to different churches e.g., 2 Corinthians 1:1. Paul is the commander and Timothy the co-worker, the Lieutenant.

Meeting Timothy reminds you of his trainers in the faith

Meeting Timothy also reminds us of his trainers in the faith—grandmother, Lois and mother, Eunice (2 Tim. 1:5), or the apostle Paul himself.

Yes, Timothy was naturally timid (1 Tim. 4:12; 2 Tim. 1:7–8) but remember those who criticised Paul's personality (2 Cor. 10:1). Investigate further and discover young Timothy to be reputable (Acts 16:2), supportive (Acts 16:5), unselfish (Acts 18:5; Phil. 2:22) and faithful (1 Cor. 4:17; 2 Tim. 1:2). It is good to be in the company of a young man who loves the Lord and his word; someone who does not care for his own interests but for those of the Lord and the Lord's people (Phil. 2:20–22).

Timothy must grasp the gospel torch

Look at this young man. Think then how vital it is that he

was willing to suffer and be committed to God's and Paul's gospel (2 Tim. 4:6–8). *There is a hope*: our younger, faithful people—like Timothy—must grasp the gospel torch to show Jesus' worth, by word and deed, to a desperate world.

Brian Wilson

Paul

Chapter 20

AN OLD MAN'S PRIORITIES:

A precious manuscript

The life of Paul is like a precious manuscript torn at both ends. When and where he was born, along with how and when he died, is not exactly known. We believe that the second Epistle to Timothy was his final correspondence to survive. Chapter four of the epistle is full of personal details and emotional requests. The situation appears to be that the aged apostle was soon expecting to face the last privilege of a Roman citizen: death by sword stroke. In verse thirteen Paul set out a list of his needs and they constitute his priorities in that crisis moment:

> When you come, bring the cloak that I left with Carpus at Troas, and my scrolls, especially the parchments (2 Tim. 4:13 NIV)

Material supplies

Paul wanted his cloak to keep himself warm in the Roman dungeon. There is nothing unspiritual in seeking earthly provisions. C.H. Spurgeon put that truth nicely: 'Although our citizenship is in heaven we have got to get by in the here and now on earth.'[1] Jesus taught us to appreciate the provision of 'daily bread' (Matt. 6:11).

Social intercourse

Paul was looking forward to the arrival of Timothy, his true son in the faith and in the field of service. Some folks think it is a mark of deep spirituality to leave unmentioned the contribution of colleagues.

It has been wisely said that it is all well and good to assert the joys of solitude just so long as you have someone to whom you can recite them.

A contemporary scholar writes:

> No medicine is more valuable, none more efficacious, none better suited to the cure of all our temporal ills than a friend to whom we may turn for consolation in time of trouble and with whom we may share our happiness in times of joy.[2]

Didn't Jesus dignify his disciples with the intensely personal designation, *'friends'* (Luke 12:4)?

Spiritual resources.

The reference to 'the parchments' is significant; Paul wanted the Scriptures which are the very words of God:

> All Scripture is God-breathed and is useful for teaching, rebuking, correcting and training in righteousness, so that the servant of God may be thoroughly equipped for every good work (2 Tim. 3:16–17 NIV).

Only the inspired Scriptures can fortify the soul when times are rough and pain is all around. Our belief in the reliability of Scripture arises, not from an ability to prove that Scripture is perfect from start to finish. Rather it rests on the witness of Jesus to the infallibility of the Scriptures. Jesus taught us that the sacred pages are authenticated by God himself. In every crisis of life, the word sustains us!

Arthur Clarke

Bibliography

Aelred of Rievaulx, *Spiritual Friendship (Cistercian Fathers 5)*, published April 4th 2007 by Cistercian Publications (first published 1974).

Barton, W.E., *The Soul of Abraham Lincoln*, (University of Illinois Pres) (2005) pp. 189–191.

Blanchard, J., *The Complete Gathered Gold: A Treasury of Quotations for Christian.* (Evangelical Press & Services Ltd; First edition 2006)

Dudley-Smith, T., *John Stott: The Making of a Leader*, (IVP, 1999) p. 97

Fernández-Armesto, F., *Francis-Drake*, (https://www.britannica.com/biography).

Graham, B., *Angels: God's Secret Agents*, (Hodder & Stoughton, 15 July 2004).

Leeman, R. W., *African-American Orators: A Bio-critical source book* (ABC-CLIO, Greenwood Press, 1996) p. 176

Endnotes

Acknowledgments

1   Quoted from: robertmorrisonproject.org

Ch. 2 Elihu

1   Benjamin Disraeli's speech at Knightsbridge (July 27,1878) resourced from https://libquotes.com/benjamin-disraeli/quote/lby3k6n

2   A body of elected elders along with their minister who govern their own congregation.

Ch. 4 Joseph

1   By permission: from a private journal of Dr Carson, in the possession of his eldest son.

Ch. 5 Moses

1   Fernández-Armesto, F., *Francis-Drake* https://www.britannica.com/biography/Francis-Drake

2   Barton, W.E. *The Soul of Abraham Lincoln*, (University of Illinois Pres) pp. 189–191.

Ch. 8 Elijah

1   Author's own translation

Ch. 11 Gabriel

1   Graham, B. *Angels: God's Secret Agents*, (Hodder & Stoughton) (15 July 2004)

Ch. 12 Simeon

1   Author's own translation

Ch. 15 Barnabas

1   Timothy Dudley-Smith, *John Stott: The Making of a Leader*, (IVP, 1999) p. 97
2   Richard W Leeman, *African-American Orators: A Bio-critical source book* (ABC-CLIO, Greenwood Press, 1996) p. 176

Ch. 20 Paul

1   Blanchard, J. *The Complete Gathered Gold: A Treasury of Quotations for Christians* (Evangelical Press, 1 Nov 2006).
2   Aelred of Rievaulx, *Spiritual Friendship* (Cistercian Fathers 5), (Yorkshire: Cistercian Publications, 2007). First published 1974.